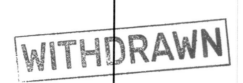

Dedicated to Helen Oliver who is very good at looking
after everyone's heads.

FEATHERSTONE
Bloomsbury Publishing Plc
50 Bedford Square, London, WC1B 3DP, UK

BLOOMSBURY, FEATHERSTONE and the Feather logo are trademarks of Bloomsbury Publishing Plc

First published in Great Britain 2019 by Bloomsbury Publishing Plc

A catalogue record for this book is available from the British Library

ISBN: HB: 978-1-4729-5923-2; ePDF: 978-1-4729-5922-5; ePub: 978-1-4729-6625-4

2 4 6 8 10 9 7 5 3 1

Printed and bound in China by Leo Paper Products, Heshan, Guangdong

All papers used by Bloomsbury Publishing Plc are natural, recyclable products from wood grown in well managed forests. The manufacturing processes conform to the environmental regulations of the country of origin.

To find out more about our authors and books visit www.bloomsbury.com and sign up for our newsletters

What's Going On Inside My Head?

Starting conversations with your child about positive mental health

Molly Potter

ILLUSTRATED BY

Sarah Jennings

FEATHERSTONE

LONDON OXFORD NEW YORK NEW DELHI SYDNEY

Dear Reader,

Our minds are where we do all our thinking. Thinking includes making decisions about what to do, deciding what to believe in and coming up with new ideas. What we think very much affects how we feel about ourselves and how well we cope with things that happen to us. Our minds and the thinking they do are therefore really important and because of this, it's crucial that we look after them and keep them as healthy as possible.

We can't just flick a switch and make our minds healthy – we have to keep working at it. Keeping a healthy mind is about becoming aware of our thoughts and how they affect us. We need to practise healthy thinking habits and find ways of coping when upsetting things happen. This book gives you lots of ideas about how to keep your mind healthy.

It's important to know...

Our brain is the organ inside our head that controls everything that happens in our body such as making our mouth move to speak and keeping our heart pumping. A brain is a solid organ and looks a bit like a sponge. Although we do all our thinking in our brains, you can't see what we call our 'minds' because they are made up of thoughts, imagination and beliefs which are not solid objects.

Contents

How should I think about myself?

Feeling good about ourselves and having positive thoughts are not always easy things to do. Sometimes we think too much about what we're not good at or we compare ourselves to others and decide we're rubbish! This is never a helpful thing to do.

He's much better than me.

Ah well, I'll try again.

Everyone is different and we all have things we're good at and things we're not so good at. We feel better about ourselves if we celebrate successes but also accept that we can't be brilliant at everything (nobody can) and this is absolutely fine.

6

Accepting yourself as you are, knowing what you're good at and what you're not so good at is a way of being kind to yourself. When you make a mistake, it's important that you forgive yourself (and hopefully learn from it so you don't make the same mistake again!). Forgiving yourself helps you keep a healthy mind.

I really like skipping.

I'm not so good at catching.

Top tip

Just because you aren't naturally brilliant at something, doesn't mean you should stop trying to get better at it. If you really want to, you can get better at anything with lots of practice. It takes bravery to stick at something you don't find easy.

How does looking after my body help my mind?

Our body carries our brain around, protects it and makes sure it has what it needs to work properly. If our body is working well, our brain is more likely to be working well too. If we do the things that we know keep our body fit and healthy, then our brain and mind are more likely to be healthy too.

It's good to know...

Sometimes when we feel a bit sad or low, exercise can make us feel so much better especially if it's outdoors in a park, a wood or in the countryside where there are trees and grass.

For a healthy body and mind, we need to make sure we...

Have enough sleep.

Drink plenty of water.

Eat plenty of fruit and vegetables.

Spend some time outside.

Do some exercise
(at least half an hour a day).

Take time to relax.

What is happiness?

People often say that it's important to be happy. However, if you ask lots of different people what they think happiness is, they will probably give you lots of different answers.

People talk about two kinds of happiness. The first is when they feel happy because something nice has just happened. This kind of happiness doesn't last for long and nobody could expect to feel this sort of happiness all the time.

The second kind of happiness is when people feel good about most of the things in their lives like their families, their friends, their homes, their hobbies and their schools or jobs. This type of happiness is something people can work at and it can last longer. When we feel this kind of happiness, our minds tend to be healthy.

What's happiness?

Things that make people happy with their lives:

Finding things you really love doing like drawing, making things or reading.

Spending time with your family, chatting, laughing and getting cuddles.

Having fun with friends (and pets!) and being kind to them.

Playing sport or being outside enjoying the fresh air.

What do I do with emotions?

When anything happens to us, we feel something inside. This feeling is also called an emotion. It might be a strong emotion or it might be weak – almost so we don't notice it. It might be an enjoyable feeling or an unenjoyable one. Emotions are all part of being a human and you can't avoid them. In fact, trying to ignore them is not a good idea. Getting good at dealing with feelings helps to keep our minds healthy.

| Scared | Happy | Annoyed | Confused | Shocked |

Sometimes when we feel negative emotions, we behave in ways that upset or hurt ourselves or other people. We can't do anything about the way we feel but we can decide how to behave, whatever emotion we are feeling.

Getting good at dealing with feelings helps us to keep our minds healthy.
Here are some questions you can ask yourself:

1. 'How am I feeling right now?' (To help you start to recognise your feelings.)

2. 'What might have made me feel this way?' (To help you understand what causes different emotions.)

3. 'What would be the best thing I could do to help me deal with what I am feeling?' (Think of things you could do that will help you feel better. There are some ideas on the next page.)

It's good to know...

Being human means you will have both positive and negative feelings. Sometimes you will go around with a big smile on your face but other times you might cry and feel sad. Different feelings come and go and this is normal. Nobody can expect to feel positive feelings all the time.

When something upsetting happens, what will help me?

Upsetting things happen to everyone now and again — like a pet dying or your parents arguing. When this happens we can feel uncomfortable feelings like anger, sadness or fear. We can't stop these feelings but there are things we can do to help deal with them. These are called coping plans.

Sometimes when we feel uncomfortable feelings, what we feel like doing at the time doesn't really help or it can even make things worse. For example, if someone was angry, they might go and play a computer game to try and forget but then realise they still feel upset when they stop playing or they might be really rude to someone they love.

For a coping plan that works well, you could...

- Talk to someone about how you feel.

- Ask for a hug and have a cry.

- Take time to sit quietly and wonder if there is anything good about what happened.

- Think about anything you might have learnt because of what happened.

- Think about a time in the future when this thing won't bother you as much.

- Go for a walk or punch a pillow to get rid of any built-up energy.

- Take time to meditate (see page 20).

- Remember to think about all the things you love.

What can I do when thoughts bother me?

Most of us have times when our minds ruminate. That's a long word! It means thinking or worrying about something and not being able to stop thinking about it. It's one of the drawbacks of having a brain! It usually happens when you believe you can't cope with something – but the chances are you totally can.

I wish I hadn't done that.

I feel *so* silly.

They must think I'm stupid.

When you ruminate, it's important firstly to recognise that a thought is doing this. Once you realise this, then it's time to put a plan in place to try and stop it bothering you so much.

You could...

Think about a time when you coped with something similar. Remember that you can probably cope with what's bothering you this time too.

Find someone to talk to about your troubling thoughts and work out together what could be done to help.

Imagine taking the annoying thought out of your head and putting it in a bucket. Put the bucket in the corner of the room and put a lid on it. Every now and then tell it to be quiet!

Use up the space in your brain with a calming thought. Close your eyes and imagine a circle with a dot drawn near the edge. The circle spins slowly so the dot goes up when you breathe in and down when you breathe out.

It's good to know...

Something that you can do to help prevent rumination so that it bothers you less is to practise really focusing on the moment you are in. To tune into 'right now', you can think about what you see, hear, smell and feel – one sense at a time.

What can I do when someone upsets me?

People can often upset other people – both children and grown-ups. Sometimes they mean to and other times they don't. When it happens we could decide to just go away and be upset. However, this is not usually the best way of dealing with it and it can mean our mind keeps thinking about what happened – which is not healthy.

I'm really upset he won't let me play.

I'm not letting him play – no way!

It is better to explain how what happened made you feel to the person who upset you. We usually feel better after we have done this. If you are lucky – you might get an apology.

When you ignored me, I felt angry.

Another good thing to do is to get good at forgiving people. To do that you have to think about what happened in a different way. Perhaps the person who upset you is jealous or maybe they are really unhappy about something that you don't know about. When you forgive someone, it's a true sign that what they did no longer bothers you.

It's important to know...

If someone keeps picking on you on purpose and you feel like you can't sort it out for yourself, this is called bullying. When this happens you need to keep telling adults about it until you get help that makes it stop.

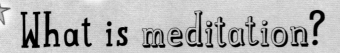

What is meditation?

Sometimes our minds can be mischievous because they make us think too much. This overthinking can make us worry about the future (which is silly because you can never know what is actually going to happen in the future). It can also make us feel bad about things that we did in the past (which is also a bit silly because we can't do anything much about the past either).

Meditation can help quieten down our minds and help us let go of the past, stop worrying too much about the future and only notice the 'now'. This can make us feel calm and peaceful which is really good for our minds.

There are lots of different ways of meditating. The more you practise the better you will get. Here are some different forms of meditation you can try:

Sit comfortably in a quiet place and close your eyes...

1. Think of a sound or word that is calming (like 'ommmm') and in your head softly say it over and over again. If your mind wanders to other thoughts, again gently go back to repeating the word over and over in your head.

Ommm...

10, 9 ,8 , 7...

2. Start at ten and slowly count down to zero with each deep breath you take. After zero, just think 'in' and 'out' in time with your breathing.

3. Imagine you are in a really wonderful place. It can be a place you know or a made-up one. Imagine what you can see, hear, feel and smell. Enjoy that space.

How do I ask for help when I need it?

Help is a good thing. When we're struggling, asking for help and getting it is a really smart thing to do. It's also true that we are more likely to get help from some people than others so it is a good plan to think about who these helpful people are before you need to ask them. These people can become your support network.

It's best to have a mixture of children and adults in your support network. A friend at school might be good at cheering you up if you're upset but if you're being bullied you would need an adult's help.

Make a list of the people in your support network. You can have as many people as you like. This helps remind you that there is always help. The more people you have, the easier it will be to find help when you need it.

22

Think about who you would ask for help if...

You were trying to do something and finding it really difficult.

Someone was picking on you.

You saw something on TV that upset you.

You felt lonely at playtime.

You were finding it difficult to go to sleep at night.

You were really worried about something you were going to do the next day.

It's important to know...

When you need help, if the first person you ask doesn't really help then keep asking different people until you get the help you need.

How do friends and family help keep my mind healthy?

Humans like to be with other humans. We are made to have relationships with each other and we mostly feel happier when we spend time doing things with friends and family. Friends and family are important for keeping our minds healthy.

Even though they are really important, relationships are not always easy and it's usual for friends and families to upset each other from time to time.

To help you remember how important friends and familiy are, think of a time when...

A member of your family helped you.

Someone in your family took you somewhere nice.

Or a time when...

A friend said something nice about you.

You spent time with a family member or friend doing something you love doing.

A friend looked really pleased to see you.

A friend stood up for you.

It's important to know...

We are unlikely to make friends with everyone we meet and this is fine. We are allowed to like some people more than others – everybody does. Fortunately, everyone finds the friends that are right for them.

How can I be a better friend?

Good friendships (and family relationships) help to support us and make us feel looked after. Getting good at relationships sometimes needs a bit of practice.

Think about when you arrive somewhere – how do you think you make the other people there feel? It's normal for some people to like you more than others but do you ever wonder about the effect your words and behaviour have on other people?

Hello everyone.

She's really funny.

Oh look, it's Miss Bossy Pants.

You can probably think of people you are always happy to see and others that you are less happy to see. Can you think why this might be?

26

We cannot change who we are but we can think about how we behave. There are some behaviours that nearly always make other people feel good and others that are likely to make them feel unhappy. When we make other people feel great, they are far more likely to be kind to us and want to be our friend which then makes us feel good.

Have a look at these behaviours. Which do you like, which don't you mind and which do you really not like?

- Giving real compliments
- Telling lies
- Listening
- Letting others join in
- Helping others when they are upset
- Boasting
- Sharing your things with others
- Laughing at and teasing others
- Showing an interest
- Being bossy
- Smiling
- Moaning lots

How can I improve my thinking habits?

In the same way as we can exercise and eat well to keep our bodies healthy, we can practise thinking in ways that help our minds stay healthy.

Here are some ideas to try:

Try to be optimistic. This means looking for the good things in any situation. For example, if you mostly don't like school, try hard to think about the bits you do like. This might include seeing your friends, playtime or art lessons.

Think positively. At the end of every day, think about the best thing that happened and remember how it made you feel.

Always try to think of kind things to do or say when you're with your friends and family.

Don't expect to get everything right all of the time. Forgive yourself when you make mistakes – after all, we all make mistakes!

It's important to know...

When something is bothering you, do something to help yourself – like using the ideas included in this book.

Guidance for parents and carers

Please note!

This book does not attempt or claim to be a resource that can be used to prevent mental illness or address mental health problems. It is a book that aims to help children develop self-awareness, consider how to look after themselves and improve their emotional literacy. It suggests ways of accessing help and support and encourages children to consider and develop helpful coping strategies – all things known to contribute to developing resilience.

If your child experiences behavioural, emotional or developmental difficulties, it is important that you seek expert advice.

Tips for supporting positive mental health and to help develop resilience

Make sure your child gets plenty of exercise (preferably outdoors)

Exercise has been shown to have a positive effect on overall health and mood. Going for a walk or run or playing a game with your child is great for your relationship and it's healthy too.

Make sure your child gets a balanced diet

The advantages of a healthy diet are increased concentration, better physical performance and less likelihood of getting ill. Encourage your child to drink plenty of water for a healthy body and brain.

Help your child to develop positive relationships

Positive relationships help us cope with difficulties and promote positive mental health. Your role-modelling of positive relationships with trust and respectful communication is likely to have the greatest impact on your child's beliefs about what relationships should look like. Encourage your child to consider what makes him or her a good (or not so good) friend and discuss what they can do when difficulties within friendships arise (see also *Will You Be My Friend?* by Molly Potter). Also help your child to appreciate how important friends and family are by asking them questions about what they do with their friends or family members each day and showing an interest.